THE SOLDIER THROUGH THE AGES

THE GREEK HOPLITE

Martin Windrow

Illustrated by
Tony Smith

WITHDRAWN

Franklin Watts
London   New York   Toronto   Sydney

© Franklin Watts Ltd 1985

First printed in Great Britain in 1985 by
Franklin Watts Ltd
12a Golden Square
London W1

First published in the USA by
Franklin Watts Inc.
387 Park Avenue South
New York
N.Y. 10016

First published in Australia by
Franklin Watts Australia
1 Campbell Street
Artarmon
NSW 2064

UK ISBN: 0 86313 154 9
US ISBN: 0-531-03780-0
Library of Congress Catalog Card Number: 84-50020

Designed by James Marks
Cover illustration by Gerry Embleton

Printed in Belgium

J
355
WLN

Contents

The cradle of civilization

The civilization which is called Classical Greece occupied the lands around the Aegean Sea in the 6th and 5th centuries BC. It was the earliest European civilization which left full written records for historians, and its art, politics, culture and its armies were far more advanced than those found anywhere else in the West.

Ancient Greece was never a single unified country. Because the countryside was mostly mountainous and wooded, there were few places where people could settle to farm good land. As a result, the towns that were built were far apart, and grew up into separate city-states, covering fairly small areas. The city-states were constantly quarreling and forming alliances in rivalry with one another. This rivalry often led to open warfare, particularly between the armies of the city-states of Athens and Sparta.

In the Classical period the infantryman was the backbone of all the armies of the different Greek states. He was called a hoplite, which means an armored man. The hoplite fought in an organized regiment of men, each of whom used the same weapons in the same way. He was given military training according to rules laid down by his government.

▷ A typical Greek heavy infantryman of the two centuries between 600 and 400 BC. The Greek hoplite wore a crested bronze helmet. His chest and back were protected by armor of metal or heavy fabric, and on his legs he wore metal greaves. He was armed with a long spear which he used for stabbing, not throwing.

The Greek hoplite was a disciplined fighter, obeying the orders of his officers, at a time when other warriors in Europe fought as loose mobs of undisciplined individuals. As far as we know, the Greek hoplite was the first European who was not just a warrior but a soldier. He and his fellow fighters were the true ancestors of today's armies.

◁ The most important Greek city-states of the 6th and 5th centuries are shown on this map. The rivalry between Athens and Sparta led to a long series of ruinous wars. In the end this so weakened them that they were ripe for invasion from the strong new kingdom of Macedonia in the north.

5

A citizen's duty

The Greek hoplite was not a full-time, paid soldier. Usually he earned his living as a farmer: rich men lived in the city and had stewards to run their estates, while poorer men worked their land themselves. All citizens, rich or poor, also played a part in running their city by voting in the city assembly. And, in times of war, rich and poor alike were expected to report for army service.

Citizens had the time for these duties because almost everyone owned slaves. These might be foreign prisoners or poor people who had been sold into slavery when they could not pay their debts. There were many more slaves than citizens, and they did all heavy work. A rich man might own as many as 1,000 slaves, and even a poor peasant farmer had two or three.

In Athens there was a third class of people, called metics. These were foreigners living in the city. They were mostly businessmen and traders. They had few political rights, but they did serve in the army. In all, Athens is believed to have had about 40,000 citizens, plus their families; 20,000 metics, and their families; and about 180,000 slaves.

▷ The three "faces" of an Athenian citizen: soldier, voter and farmer. Every healthy male citizen was expected to serve in the army whenever he was needed. The Greeks believed that if a man enjoyed the advantages of living in a city, then he should be prepared to fight to defend it.

The citizen was also expected to attend the city assembly regularly – perhaps three times a month – and to help run the city by electing officials and passing laws.

Most farmers did not have enough flat land to grow much grain. Instead they grew grapes for wine, and olives, the two crops that made Athens rich. They also grew many different kinds of vegetables.

△ For every eight citizens of Athens (top), there were about four metics, (middle), and twelve slaves (bottom). The Athenian army in about 430 BC was made up of about 13,000 citizen hoplites; 9,500 metics; 1,400 young cadets; 2,500 veterans in their 50s, and 1,000 wealthy men on horseback – a total of 27,400 men.

Every man an athlete

A Greek boy's education was decided by his father. Usually he was sent to take lessons at the house of a paid teacher, often accompanied by one of his father's slaves, who made sure he did not play truant! In a small class of other boys, he was taught reading, writing, poetry, arithmetic and music.

In a country where every man was a part-time soldier, and at a time when soldiers fought with heavy iron-bladed weapons, it was important for each boy to grow up strong and agile. From about the age of twelve Greek boys were sent for regular training at an athletics school.

The school had an open-air training ground surrounded by changing-rooms, baths and offices. The earth of the training ground was regularly dug, raked and watered to keep it soft. Here, under the eye of the instructor, boys practiced fitness exercises, jumping, wrestling, throwing the discus and javelin, and boxing. (Boxing in ancient Greece was a tough sport, since the boxers used heavy straps wrapped round their fists instead of today's padded gloves.)

After his education was completed, the young Greek man still took part in sports to keep himself in shape. In wartime his life would depend on his strength, endurance and quick reflexes.

▷ Greek boys practicing at an athletics school. The instructors wore purple robes and carried forked sticks. Flute-players helped the boys keep in time. For some exercises the boys carried weights to improve their strength and balance. When they wrestled, they covered themselves with oil and sand for grip. Each boy took his oil pot to school with him – and sponges and metal scrapers so that he could clean off this mess in the baths afterwards!

Military service

When he was eighteen, every Athenian boy reported for two years' full-time military training as a cadet. The cadets were formed into units according to their home district. Whenever he was called up for army service in later life, the soldier served in this same unit, made up of neighbors and friends of his own age. Officers were elected by the district's voters from among trusted veterans.

For the first year the cadets, dressed in special black cloth tunics, lived in barracks just outside Athens. First they were taught how to handle their weapons, wear their armor, and drill together. Since their families had to buy their armor, there was a good deal of difference from man to man.

During that first year the cadets were taken to all the important fortresses in the country so that they would know their way around if they ever had to defend them in wartime. At the end of the year the cadets put on a grand parade and drill display, and each one was presented by the city authorities with a shield and spear to mark his graduation.

For the second year the cadets garrisoned forts around the frontiers. Life was probably pleasant enough: they were used to exercise, an open-air life and a simple diet. (Most Greeks ate barley bread, with cheese, fish, olives, onions and other vegetables, and pork or goat for special occasions.)

The cadet returned to private life when he was twenty; but he could be recalled to the army in wartime at any time up to his sixtieth birthday. Men in their fifties were called up to garrison the forts alongside the cadets. Although the part-time citizen-soldier was given no pay for his service, he received free medical attention if he was wounded, and a public pension.

▷ A young Athenian hoplite is helped into his armor by his father and brothers. His age-group has been called up for service with his district regiment. He will serve with the main army. His father and his younger brother – who wears the black tunic of a cadet – will serve as fort guards.

10

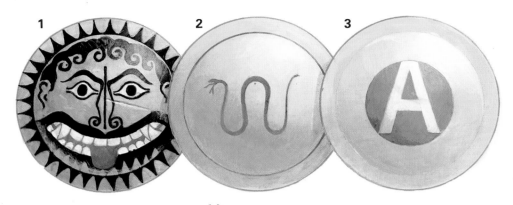

◁ The beautiful shield markings probably identified units, as well as being decorative. There were many types, including:
1 Gods or demons.
2 Real or imaginary animals.
3 Symbols or initial letters of city names.

The hoplite's equipment

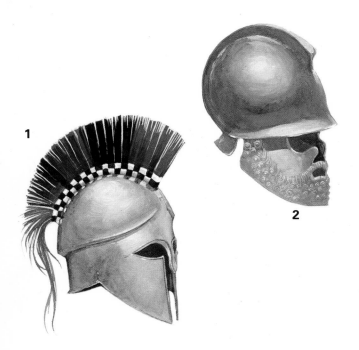

1

2

Helmets came in many styles, but most were bronze and covered the head except for narrow slots for the eyes, nose and mouth. As the metal was thin and springy, the helmet could be pushed up on top of the head when not in battle. Helmets were often embossed or painted for decoration, and were fitted with horsehair crests.

The hoplite wore a cuirass to protect his chest and back. In the 6th century BC this

◁ **1, 2** Two common helmet types, the Corinthian and Thracian. The latter has a beard embossed on the face-piece for decoration.

▽ **3** "Muscled" cuirass. **4** Linen cuirass; metal plates were sometimes added for extra protection. The cloth was about $\frac{1}{4}$ in (0.5 cm) thick.

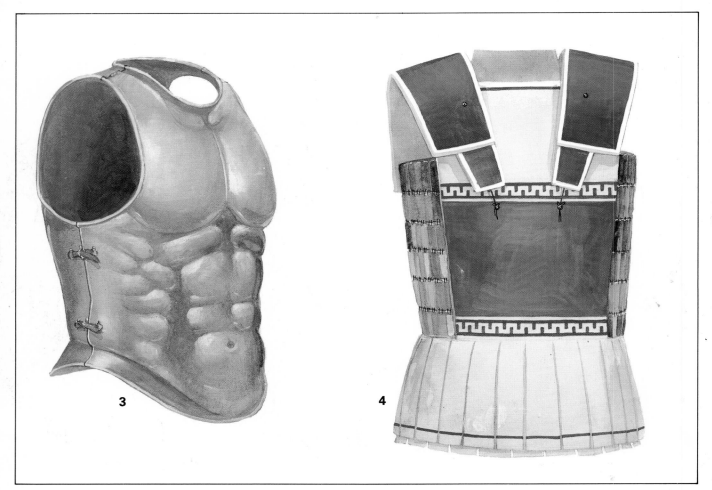

3

4

was bronze and "muscled" like a human torso. This elegant but expensive armor was later replaced by a simpler version made of layers of stiff cloth glued together. The legs were protected by greaves, flexible metal shin guards.

The hoplite carried a round shield made of wood covered with bronze which measured about 2 ft 7 in (80 cm) across. Its inturned rim rested on his shoulder, taking some of the weight off his arm.

His main weapon was a long ash-wood spear with an iron blade. Often it had a spike at the butt end, to be used if the spear was broken in battle. Various types of short swords were also carried for close fighting.

▽ **5** Greaves, split up the back to fit around the legs.
6, 7 Inside and outside of the shield. A leather curtain was sometimes attached to stop arrows aimed at the legs.
8 Spear, between 5 and 8 ft (1.5 m–2.5 m) long.
9 The usual type of double-edged sword, about 2 ft (60 cm) long.
10 Another type of sword, the single-edged kopis, used like a cleaver.

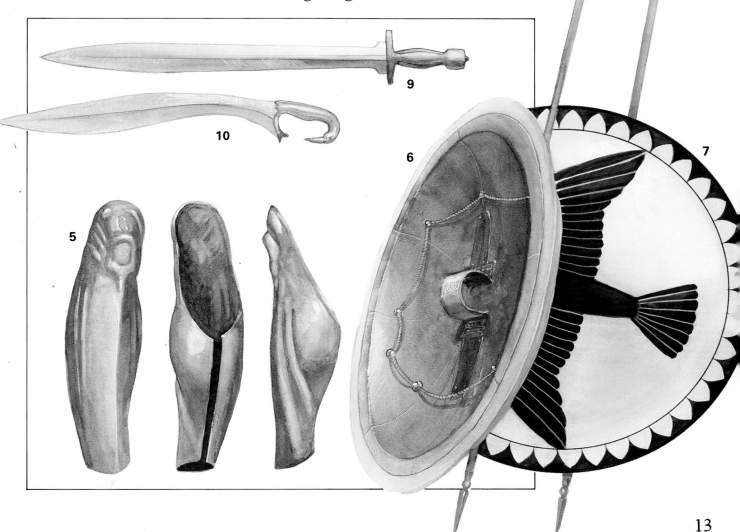

Battle formation

The Greeks fought in tight-packed formations, so it was important for the hoplite to learn how to handle his awkward spear and shield without getting in his comrades' way. The diagram on the right shows the basic formation: a company of 100 men, drawn up 8 deep by 12 wide.

The smallest unit was the single file of 8 men, one behind the other. The senior man in each file stood at the front. Three files made up a platoon of 25 men (red, yellow, blue, brown). The extra, 25th, man was an experienced veteran, who stood behind the platoon to keep an eye on the men. The platoon commanders (the large colored figures) stood at the front of their right-hand file. The four platoons made up the company.

In battle the army used a very simple formation called the phalanx. All the 100-man companies simply stood side by side, in a long line 8 ranks deep. In a big battle the phalanx might be $1\frac{1}{4}$ miles (2 km) long from end to end.

▷ Hoplites in typical fighting positions:
1 Crouched behind the shield, sheltering against arrows.
2 Standing in the battle-line, thrusting underarm with the spear.
3 Thrusting overarm, perhaps over the shoulder of the man in front. The phalanx was too tightly packed for any more complicated movements.

1

2

3

Battle tactics

The important thing about the Greek hoplite was that he fought not just for himself, but as one of a team. The tactics of the phalanx worked because each soldier kept in his allotted place, acting together with his comrades, according to orders. This discipline held the phalanx together, so that each soldier could take advantage of opportunities to help the men on each side of him.

When two Greek armies met in battle, the lines were drawn up some distance apart. After the commanders had whipped up their men's courage with inspiring speeches, trumpets sounded the advance. To the sound of flutes and war songs, each mass of spearmen marched toward the other. At the last moment they broke into a run, and two opposing front ranks crashed together, shield to shield.

Each man stabbed with his spear, trying to reach past the shields of the men facing him. The men behind stabbed over the shoulders of the front rank. Those too far back to reach pushed on the backs of the men in front, or passed extra spears forward to them.

▷ The spearman's helmet covered most of his face. His shield covered his body from chin to thigh, and greaves protected his legs. But his right side was partly exposed to a spear thrust when he raised his right arm to stab downward with his own spear. For this reason, he tended to tuck himself well in behind the edge of the shield of the man on his right.

16

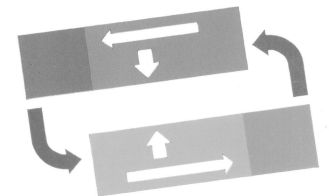

△ This is what often happened in a Greek battle. Each army usually put its best men at the right-hand end of its battle-line, so they often pushed back the weaker troops facing them. As both wings pushed forward, the whole battle started to turn counterclockwise.

Soldiers in both armies gradually shuffled to their right, trying to keep behind the shields of the men on their right. So the right-hand end of each battle-line soon overlapped the weaker left-hand end of the enemy line, and attacked it from the flank.

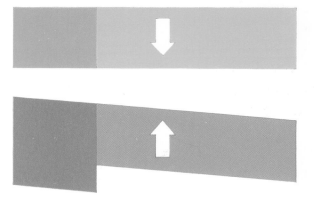

△ This is how a Theban general beat the Spartans at the Battle of Leuctra in 371 BC. The Thebans (green) advanced in a slanted line. Their best men were placed on the left, not on the right as usual; and they were drawn up in many more ranks than the rest of the army. So the strongest part of the Theban army hit the Spartans first; and, having so many ranks, they were able to beat the best of the Spartans. By the time the rest of the Theban line closed in on them, the Spartans were already crumbling.

Face to face across the spears

Two Greek armies crash together in the first moment of battle. Once the rigid lines of spearmen were locked in combat, there was little room for maneuver or cunning. The battle was decided by a vicious, face-to-face killing-match. This did not usually last long. Many of the officers, fighting in the front rank, fell early in the battle. Their men would be shaken; and once it was clear which side was winning, the losers often gave up and ran for their lives. They were usually allowed to get away. Once the victory had been won on the battlefield, it was thought dishonorable to hunt down beaten men and butcher them.

◁ Two armies locked in battle. As each man fell, the man behind stepped forward into his place. Eventually, one army would wear right through; as soon as the phalanx was broken, it was lost. Battles were savage, although brief. An army of 4,000 men might be left with 1,000 dead.

On the flanks

The Greek hoplite, in his rigid phalanx, was very successful in war – so long as his enemy was another Greek spearman fighting in the same way. But armies often had to march through mountains or forests, where the spearmen could not easily form up in their tight ranks. So light supporting troops were often used as well, both to raid and ambush enemies, and to guard against such attacks.

Some of these light troops were recruited from poor citizens who could not afford hoplite armor and weapons. All they needed were javelins – throwing spears – and perhaps light shields of wicker and leather. Often Greek cities hired foreign mercenaries, soldiers who would fight for whoever paid them. Various neighboring peoples became famous for their skills with different weapons, and were hired for that reason.

Thracians made good peltasts – agile, light-armed javelin-men. Archers were recruited on the island of Crete; and the island of Rhodes was famous for its slingers. Their simple, cheap leather slings could hurl a stone or lead bullet up to 380 yd (350 m) with deadly effect.

The Greek cities had few cavalry, so for scouting round their armies they hired mercenary horsemen. The best horse-archers were the Scythians. These were wild, nomadic tribesmen from the great plains north of the Black Sea. The flat countryside of Thessaly and Boeotia was also good for horse-breeding, and provided the Greeks with another type of cavalry, who used javelins.

▷ Different types of light mercenary troops watch from a hilltop as their main army enters a mountain pass.
1 Thracian peltasts took their name from the pelta, a crescent-shaped wickerwork shield.
2 Scythian horse-archers wore loose, brightly patterned tunics and trousers. Bows and arrows were carried together in a case slung from the belt.
3 Red tunics were the mark of the Cretan archers.
4 Light horsemen from Thessaly could be recognized by their broad sunhats and gaudy, patterned cloaks.

The Spartan legend

The Greek city-state of Sparta was quite unlike all the others. The Spartans became legendary as the finest soldiers in the Greek world, and were feared and respected far and wide. We still use the word "Spartan" to describe tough people who bear hardship without complaint.

Spartan life was devoted to the military virtues of courage, strength and endurance. Sparta was a grim, uncomfortable place ruled by brutal laws, and Spartans scorned all the gentle and pleasant things of life. Even their food was a test of endurance – their most famous dish was a disgusting broth made from blood and vinegar!

The Spartan citizen had only one trade: war. He was given a state-owned farm to support himself, but he never actually worked on his land. All work except soldiering was done by the local peasants called helots, who lived in cruel slavery. This allowed Spartan citizens to concentrate on a full-time military life.

From the age of seven to the age of sixty, a Spartan belonged to the army. He was taken from his mother as a little boy, and put into cold, uncomfortable barracks with other boys of his age. He lived with these companions all his life. Together they moved up through the classes of a harsh training system. At twenty they were taken into the army proper, but they were not allowed to vote, or to marry, until they were thirty.

▷ A Spartan warrior encourages two boys to fight during a winter training run. The proud marks of the warrior were the red cloak, and long, carefully dressed hair. The Spartan boy was treated harshly. He was educated only enough to understand simple written orders and to sing marching songs. All the rest of his training was devoted to building up his strength, courage and cunning. He was given only a single tunic, winter and summer, and when he was older he often went naked. His hair was cropped, and he was seldom allowed to bathe. His rations were small and unappetizing. This was to encourage him to steal and to be cunning; but if he was caught he was whipped for carelessness. At 16 he faced harsh tests of endurance. He was turned out alone to live as best he could in the wild; and finally, he had to stalk and murder a slave.

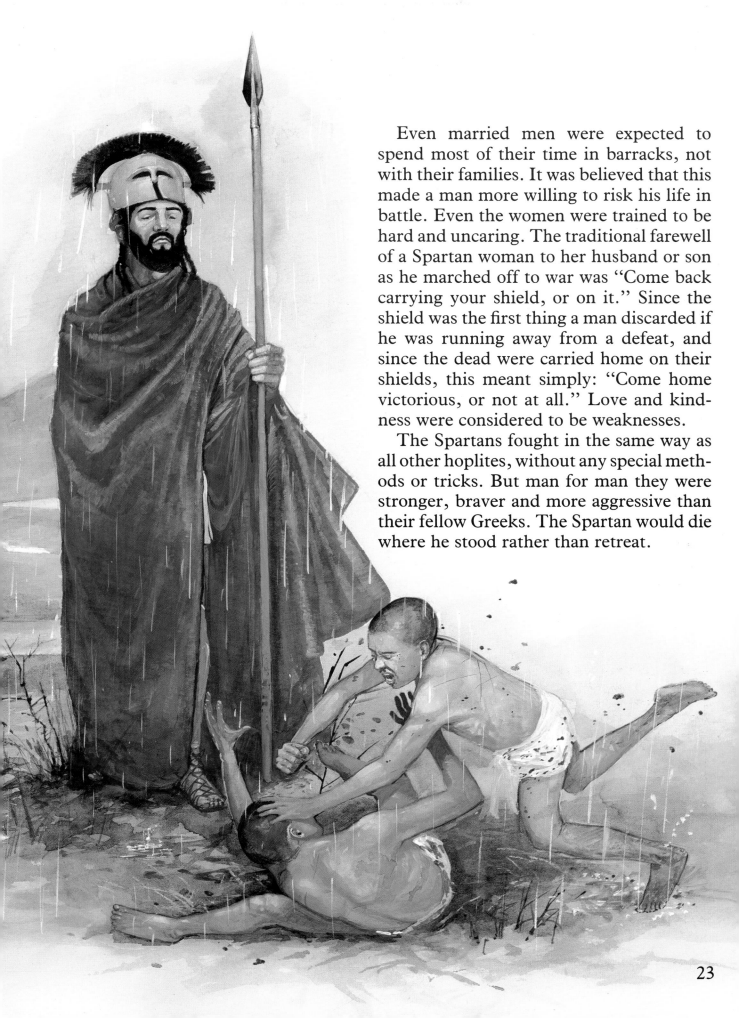

Even married men were expected to spend most of their time in barracks, not with their families. It was believed that this made a man more willing to risk his life in battle. Even the women were trained to be hard and uncaring. The traditional farewell of a Spartan woman to her husband or son as he marched off to war was "Come back carrying your shield, or on it." Since the shield was the first thing a man discarded if he was running away from a defeat, and since the dead were carried home on their shields, this meant simply: "Come home victorious, or not at all." Love and kindness were considered to be weaknesses.

The Spartans fought in the same way as all other hoplites, without any special methods or tricks. But man for man they were stronger, braver and more aggressive than their fellow Greeks. The Spartan would die where he stood rather than retreat.

The wooden walls of Athens

An important part of Athens' wealth in peace, and her strength in war, came from her large fleet – the so-called wooden walls of Athens. Athens built up a trading empire scattered all over the islands and coasts of the eastern Mediterranean. The merchant ships which used the trade routes provided the city with thousands of skilled sailors and oarsmen to man warships in times of trouble. These seamen and oarsmen were free citizens of the poorer classes, not slaves.

Greek warships were called galleys. They were long and slim, and powered mainly by banks of oars along the sides. They had a single square sail on a mast, but this was lowered before battle. The Greeks used oars to carry out maneuvers, rather than relying on the changeable wind near the shore, where most battles were fought. The oarsmen, arranged on three levels, pulled the ship along at speeds of about $5\frac{1}{2}$ mph (9 km/h). Each ship carried 170 oarsmen, 15 crew to manage the sail, anchor and steering-oars and about 16 hoplites and archers.

In battle, the tactic was to ram an enemy ship with the long, strengthened "beak" fitted low on the bows. Sometimes this was enough to sink the enemy ship, for galleys were not very strongly built. If the enemy stayed afloat, the hoplites and archers leaped across to the enemy's deck to fight hand-to-hand. In emergencies the sailors and oarsmen probably helped out too, wielding daggers and clubs.

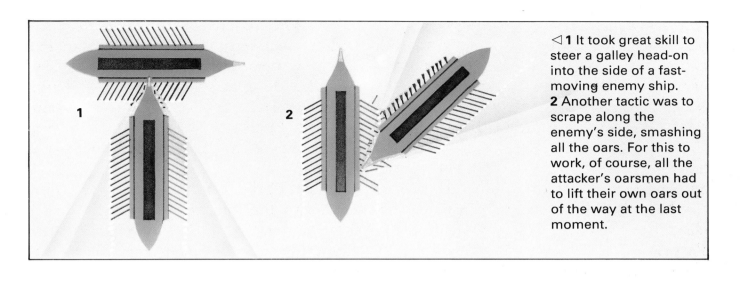

1 It took great skill to steer a galley head-on into the side of a fast-moving enemy ship.
2 Another tactic was to scrape along the enemy's side, smashing all the oars. For this to work, of course, all the attacker's oarsmen had to lift their own oars out of the way at the last moment.

▽ Greek and Persian galleys fighting each other in the Battle of Salamis, 480 BC. Athens put 200 ships into battle in this important victory – more than all other Greek navies added together.

Siege warfare

Greek armies of the 6th and 5th centuries BC used fairly simple methods to besiege an enemy city or fortress. First they built a circle of wooden fences and deep trenches all around it to cut off outside help and food supplies. Then the attackers settled down behind these ramparts and waited for the city to surrender. Often they simply bribed a traitor to open the gates.

If the Greeks decided to attack a fortified town, they raised great mounds of logs and earth against the outside of the walls. These provided ramps for storming parties to reach the top of the walls. Battering rams were sometimes used to break down the walls, and fire-arrows were aimed at wooden gates.

By the 4th century BC armies began to employ more powerful siege-machines. Great wooden catapults, powered by thick springs of twisted rope, were used to hurl stones at city walls. Battering rams were

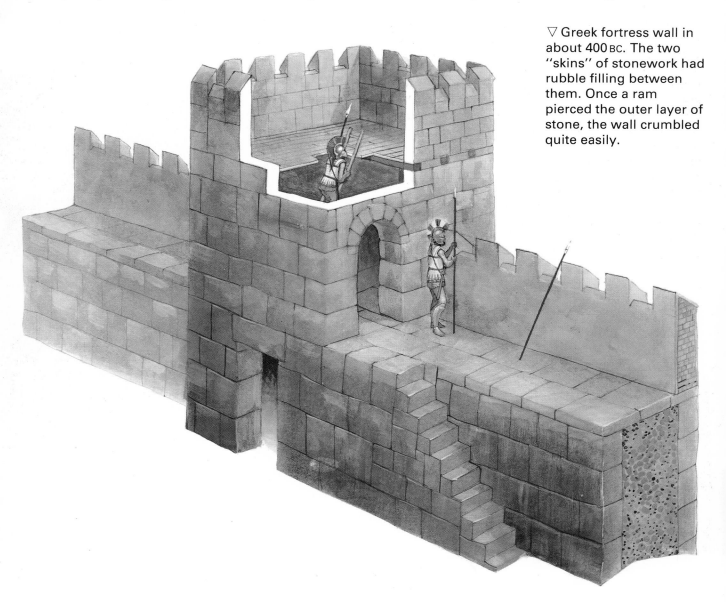

▽ Greek fortress wall in about 400 BC. The two "skins" of stonework had rubble filling between them. Once a ram pierced the outer layer of stone, the wall crumbled quite easily.

now much larger and were enclosed in a wooden framework like a shed. Protected from stones and fire-arrows by layers of padding and wet hides, they could be wheeled up to the walls. Gangs of soldiers swung the ram back and forth against the wall, safe under cover from the defenders' missiles. Tall siege towers, like moving forts, were pushed against the fortifications, and attackers clambered across from the tower on to the ramparts.

▽ A 4th-century battering ram, covered with brushwood padding and wet rawhide. The metal-headed beam swung on ropes from a strong frame. Sometimes defenders dropped heavy logs to snap off the neck of the beam where it stuck out in front. Sometimes they dangled nooses over the wall to catch the head of the ram and pull the shed over.

▷ Some siege towers were as tall as 115 ft (35 m), with ten floors connected inside by ladders. Light catapults fired through hatches, and archers manned the outside galleries. The barrage of stones and arrows forced the defenders off their ramparts, while attack-parties climbed the ladders under cover. The towers were pushed along on rollers.

The Macedonian conquerors

In 360 BC, as the weakened city-states of Greece continued their endless wrangles, a ruthless, energetic young king took the throne of Macedonia. Philip II built up a superb army and embarked on a series of campaigns against the Greek city-states. He finally defeated them in 338 BC at the Battle of Chaeronea and became master of Greece. Two years later he was succeeded by his son Alexander. Within twelve years Alexander the Great had won an immortal name as one of the world's great conquerors.

The Macedonian army of the 4th century BC was in many ways an improvement over the old phalanx. At the heart of the army was still the armored spearman standing in a massed formation. But this formation was now much stronger and deeper. The Macedonians used a battalion 16 men wide by 16 men deep, which could attack with much greater weight than the old 8-deep phalanx.

Instead of a stabbing spear, which left all but the front two or three ranks of the phalanx out of reach of the fighting, the Macedonians used a huge pike, up to 20 ft 8 in (6.3 m) long. When the soldiers held these pikes out in front of them, the heads of the first five ranks of pikes stuck out beyond the formation in a wicked steel hedge; it was impossible for any enemy with shorter weapons to get near the soldiers.

Another and most important change made by the Macedonians was the introduction of strong cavalry forces. Macedonia was flatter country than southern Greece, and good horses were bred on its plains.

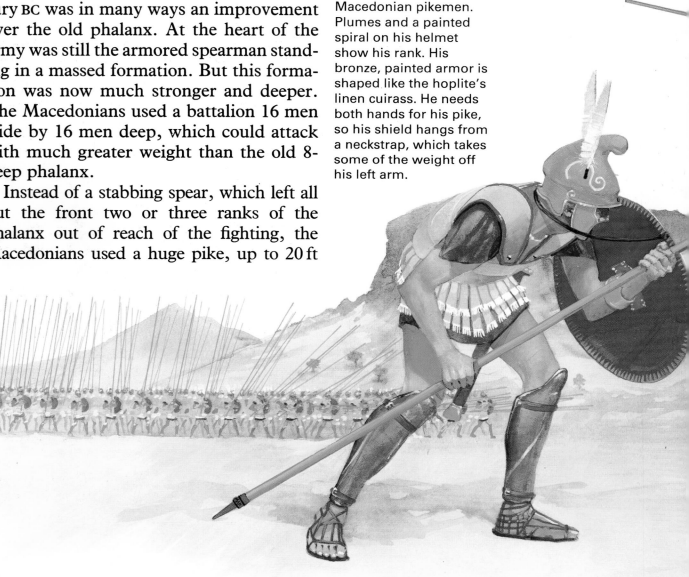

▽ Junior officer of Macedonian pikemen. Plumes and a painted spiral on his helmet show his rank. His bronze, painted armor is shaped like the hoplite's linen cuirass. He needs both hands for his pike, so his shield hangs from a neckstrap, which takes some of the weight off his left arm.

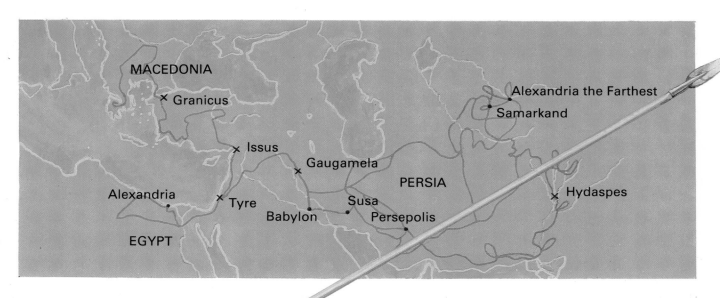

MACEDONIA

× Granicus

× Issus

Gaugamela
×

PERSIA

Alexandria the Farthest

Samarkand

Alexandria

× Tyre

Babylon

Susa

Persepolis

Hydaspes
×

EGYPT

◁ A Thessalian cavalry officer of Alexander's army. His rank is shown by the silver wreath on his helmet and by his panther-skin saddle cloth.

△ Route of Alexander's armies. In just 12 years Alexander conquered the whole Greek world, the Middle East, and western Asia as far as southern Russia and the borders of India. Many of the lessons taught by his success were remembered by the Romans who rose to power in this region 150 years later.

Philip and Alexander raised many regiments of cavalry from the Macedonian noblemen and their ranch-hands.

The riders were armored like infantrymen and armed with long lances. They were trained to ride in disciplined formations and to charge enemy infantry and cavalry on the battlefield, instead of making the hit-and-run attacks usual in those days. Alexander often led his own Companion Cavalry regiment in person at the head of its wedge-shaped formation.

Alexander's army was a balanced mixture of heavy and light infantry and cavalry, many recruited among the Asian peoples he defeated.

Glossary

Boeotia Region of Greece around the city of Thebes; its flat plains were used for growing grain crops and raising horses.

Cadet A young soldier under training.

City-state An independent community in ancient Greece – a large town and its surrounding farmlands. Small towns were usually forced to band together in alliances under the leadership of large, powerful states like Athens and Sparta.

Crete Island in the eastern Mediterranean, famous in ancient times for its skilled archers.

Cuirass Armor covering a man's chest and back down to the waist.

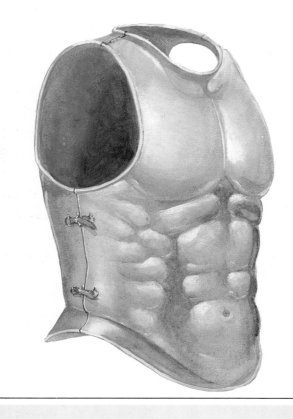

Galley Long, narrow ship mainly powered by oarsmen sitting on benches all along the sides. Ancient galleys also had a mast and sail, for cruising when the wind was favorable.

Greaves Curved pieces of armor, shaped like gutters, which protected the shins.

Helot Slave in Sparta. Helots did all farming and other work, leaving Spartan citizens free for full-time soldiering.

Hoplite Ancient Greek armored spearman: from the word *hoplon*, a shield.

Javelin Light spear, used for throwing at the enemy.

Kopis Type of ancient Greek sword. It had a heavy, slightly curved blade sharpened on one side only, and was used with a chopping stroke.

Metic Term meaning a non-Athenian free Greek man given permission to settle in Athens. Metics took care of much of the city's trade and commerce, for Athenians were snobbish about making a living by business.

Peltast A lightly armed, unarmored Greek soldier, so-called from the pelta, a light wickerwork shield which he used. Peltasts were usually either foreign mercenaries, or citizens too poor to afford a hoplite's armor.

Phalanx The massed formation of armored spearmen used by all ancient Greek armies.

Rhodes Island in the southeast Aegean Sea, famous in ancient times for its skilled slingers.

Scythians Nomadic people who lived in ancient times on the plains north of the Black Sea; they were famous for their skill as horsemen and bowmen.

Slave A person legally owned by another; a life-long bond-servant, without individual rights. Slavery was known throughout the ancient world, and all ancient economies were based upon it.

Slingers Men who used slings for hunting or fighting. A stone, or a specially made bullet of clay or metal, was whirled round the head in a leather pocket on two strings, then released at high speed. Ancient slingers were so accurate that they were said to be able to hit a charging bull on whichever horn they aimed at. Sling-stones killed at hundreds of yards' range, and could even crush a metal helmet.

Thessaly Region in the far north of Greece, where horses were bred in ancient times.

Thrace Region now known as Bulgaria; in ancient times, a wild frontier area inhabited by fierce hill tribes, who often hired out as mercenaries.

498 BC Greek colonies in Asia Minor rebel unsuccessfully against Darius, king of Persia, helped by Greek mainland states.

490 BC Darius invades Greece; Persians defeated by Athenians at Marathon.

480 BC Darius's son Xerxes invades Greece once more. Spartan force, under Leonidas, wiped out at Thermopylae after heroic resistance. Athenian and allied navies destroy Persian fleet off Salamis.

479 BC Greek victories over Persians at Plataea and Mycale end Persian threat.

478 BC Athens forms Delian League, leading alliance of 100 states in rivalry to Sparta's Peloponnesian League. For the next 70 years, constant unrest and occasional open warfare between shifting Athenian and Spartan alliances.

457 BC Pericles of Athens completes fortification of Athens and its port, Piraeus.

418 BC Sparta defeats several rebellious ex-allies at 1st Battle of Mantinea.

414 BC Disastrous defeat of Athenian army at Syracuse in Sicily.

406 BC Athenian fleet destroyed by Spartans at Aegospotami. Athens besieged, and surrenders. Sparta now overlord of Greece.

394 BC Sparta defeats rebellious Athens, Thebes and Corinth.

371 BC Epaminondas of Thebes defeats Spartans at Leuctra. A short period of Theban domination follows.

354 BC King Philip II of Macedon begins his campaigns of expansion.

338 BC Philip defeats Athens and Thebes at Chaeronea, and becomes overlord of Greece.

336 BC Philip assassinated; Alexander the Great comes to throne of Macedon and leadership of Greek world.

Index